I0446144

Duchamp-isms

Marcel Duchamp

Edited by Larry Warsh

Introduction, Selection of Quotations, and
Chronology by Francis M. Naumann

PRINCETON UNIVERSITY PRESS
Princeton and Oxford

in association with
No More Rulers

Published by Princeton University Press
41 William Street, Princeton, New Jersey 08540
99 Banbury Road, Oxford OX2 6JX

press.princeton.edu
in association with
No More Rulers
nomorerulers.com
ISMs is a trademark of No More Rulers, Inc.

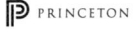 PRINCETON   NO MORE RULERS ®

GPSR Authorized Representative: Easy Access System Europe - Mustamäe tee 50, 10621 Tallinn, Estonia, gpsr.requests@easproject.com

All Rights Reserved

ISBN 9780691274485
Library of Congress Control Number: 2025936044

British Library Cataloging-in-Publication Data is available
This book has been composed in Joanna MT
Printed in China

1 3 5 7 9 10 8 6 4 2

CONTENTS

FOREWORD vii

INTRODUCTION ix

Philosophies of Art 1

Painting 21

Dada and Surrealism 35

The Readymades 45

Chess 59

Literary Influences 67

Commercialism in Art 73

Philosophies of Life and Death 83

SOURCES 106

CHRONOLOGY 119

ACKNOWLEDGMENTS 128

FOREWORD

Marcel Duchamp's singular mind challenged not only art but the very nature of thought. He believed that art is about ideas, not objects, and he expressed that belief in what he called "ready-mades"—bold gestures that included mounting a bicycle wheel on a kitchen stool, or placing a urinal on a pedestal in a gallery, and calling them both art. Duchamp has inspired generations of artists and undoubtedly will continue to do so. He was a master of his moment, and his thinking continues to influence the course of art history.

Duchamp's words, like his art, are provocative, sometimes cryptic, and often playful. In this collection of quotes, the voice of the artist comes through clearly, giving us a more complete understanding of who he was and what he thought. I invite you to explore these quotes in the spirit of Duchamp—with curiosity, a sense of humor, and a willingness to rethink the familiar. For Duchamp, that rethinking was the ground of art itself.

LARRY WARSH

JUNE 2025

INTRODUCTION

Bravo for your 60 ism-packed years.
Bravo pour vos 60 ans pleins d'ismes.[1]
—Marcel Duchamp

The quotations from Marcel Duchamp that
appear in this book were selected from the artist's public statements—primarily interviews,
the first dating from just after his arrival in
New York in 1915 and the last conducted just a

1 Telegram from Duchamp to *Art News* for their 60th anniver-
   sary issue, which they published in their December 1962 issue
   (vol. 61, no. 8, p. 26). The quotation is provided in Michel
   Sanouillet, *Salt Seller: The Writings of Marcel Duchamp* (New York:
   Oxford University Press, 1973), 161, and in Gough-Cooper
   and Caumont, *Duchamp: Work and Life / Éphémérides*, December
   8, 1962. I am grateful to Michael R. Taylor for having drawn
   this quotation to my attention.

few months before his death in 1968. Most of the early interviews were with journalists who spoke French, as Duchamp did not speak English when he arrived. Nevertheless, he quickly absorbed the rudiments of the language and began conversing—although somewhat haltingly—within a matter of months. In most cases, he answered questions with brief but factually accurate responses. Since English was not his native language, there is no question that throughout his life, he found it easier to answer more complicated and philosophically oriented questions in French.

From the first interview to the last, Duchamp was repeatedly asked questions about his painting *Nude Descending a Staircase* (Philadelphia Museum of Art; Arensberg Collection), especially by American journalists, as it had created such a sensation when it was shown at the

Armory Show in New York in 1913. After Duchamp published his notes for *The Large Glass* in 1936, questions—this time by primarily French interviewers—shifted to that complex work. His responses were intentionally omitted in the present compilation, as his comments on specific works of art can be found in countless books on the artist. Since *The Large Glass* was intentionally left incomplete, and Duchamp never returned to painting, many interviewers asked why he stopped painting. Several of his responses are shared here, articulating his distaste for painting as a profession and for its role in society—particularly how it became contaminated by its involvement with the world of finance.

Most art historians today would state that Duchamp's single greatest contribution to the art of the twentieth century was his introduction of the readymade, which occurred within months of his arrival to the United States. Although he had already made *Bicycle Wheel* (1913) and selected *Bottle Rack* (1914) back in Paris, these objects were not considered works of art until Duchamp saw the word "readymade" in a shop window in New York on a sign advertising garments that were ready-to-wear (*prêt-à-porter*). He seized upon this word to categorize the various manufactured objects that he selected and designated as works of art. However important his introduction of the readymade might have been at the time, no journalists thought to ask him questions about it until the early 1960s, some fifty years after it had been introduced—because, as Duchamp himself explained, most of the readymades disappeared and were quickly forgotten. The reason for the newfound attention was the emergence of Pop Art, with artists like Robert Rauschenberg, Jasper Johns, Roy Lichtenstein, Andy Warhol, and Claes Oldenburg using everyday objects derived from popular culture as art. The readymade was quickly identified as a critical precedent to their work.

Whenever Duchamp was asked a question about art and chess, he willingly responded, as he knew that his identity as a chess player would contribute significantly to his refutation of the old French adage *bête comme un peintre* (stupid like a painter), a notion he was devoted to dispelling. At first he explained that the game of chess was just like a drawing, in that the lines created on a chessboard could be considered as beautiful as those visible in any great work of visual art. As time passed, he even tried to get those who interviewed him to accept the fact that since he was both an artist and a chess player, the games he played should be considered art. If they accepted this supposition, he argued, then it was an art form that should be elevated above all others, as you could make no money from it, thereby removing it from the contaminating force that he felt ruined virtually everything in the art world.

When Duchamp was asked to speak publicly in the early 1950s he refused, but over the years he relented and gave several public presentations, including a lecture on his theory of the creative act, remarks prepared for the various symposia in which he participated at museums and universities, and a talk for the New York State Chess Federation. In the end, however, it was the more than sixty-five interviews that he permitted in the last decade of his life—when he was lauded as a celebrity in the art worlds of France and America—from which the majority of quotations in this book are drawn. In one of these interviews, he told a journalist that his art represents an effort to get away from himself, which he characterized as a little game between "I" and "me."[2] In another, he used similar language to assert that he was not afraid of his remarks being misconstrued. "Even if I don't believe there's too much in what I say," he said, "I don't mind even being made a fool of myself by myself."[3]

FRANCIS M. NAUMANN

JUNE 2025

2 Katherine Kuh, *The Artist's Voice: Talks with Seventeen Artists* (New York: Harper & Row, 1962), 83.

3 Interview with Colette Roberts, Spring 1963; transcript in the Alexina and Marcel Duchamp Papers, Philadelphia Museum of Art, 14.

Philosophies of Art

Art, in essence, is an outlet towards regions beyond time and space. (14)

———

Mere details of execution do not constitute the real spirit of art. (4)

———

Art can never be adequately defined, because the translation of an aesthetic emotion into a verbal description is as inaccurate as your description of fear when you have been actually scared. (18)

———

I am interested in what there is to do,
not in what I have done. (3)

———

My methods are constantly changing.
My most recent work is utterly unlike
anything that preceded it. (4)

———

Art is all a matter of personality. (4)

———

In art for all, we mean that everybody is
welcome to look freely at all works of art and
try to hear what I call an aesthetic echo. (18)

———

Generally speaking, very few people are capable of an aesthetic emotion or an aesthetic echo. While many people have taste, only a few are equipped with aesthetic receptivity. (18)

———

The blending of taste with the word "art" is, for me, a mistake. Art is something much more profound than the taste of a period. (42)

———

If you refuse to imitate yourself, I mean after you have done something, then it stays as a thing by itself. But if it is repeated a number of times it becomes a taste. (28)

———

Taste is a source of pleasure and art is not a source of pleasure. It's a source which has no color, no taste. (42)

———

I tried—I don't intend to say that I succeeded—to suppress the idea of taste and the idea of attraction. (69)

———

I could live with the worst calendar picture, and with any sort of furniture, because I never put taste in my life. ... Bad, good, or indifferent, it doesn't come in. I am against interior decorators. (60)

———

If only America would realize that the art of Europe is finished—dead—and that America is the country of the art of the future, instead of trying to base everything she does on European traditions. (2)

———

The word "art" interests me very much. If it comes from Sanskrit, as I've heard, it signifies "making." Now everyone makes something, and those who make things on a canvas, with a frame, they're called artists. Formerly, they were called craftsmen, a term I prefer. (68)

———

Criticism against Modern Art is a natural consequence of the freedom given to the artist to express his individualistic view. Moreover, I consider the barometer of opposition a healthy indication of the depth of individual expression: the more hostile the criticism, the more encouraged the artists should be. (18)

———

It is a matter of indifference to me what criticism is printed in the papers and the magazines. I am simply working out my own ideas in my own way. (4)

———

I have a very definite theory ... that a work
of art exists only when the spectator has
looked at it. Until then, it's only something
that has been done but might disappear, and
nobody would know about it. And the spectator consecrates it by saying "this is good,
we'll keep it." And the spectator, in this
case, becomes posterity. (37)

———

It's always based on two poles, the
onlooker and the maker, and the spark that
comes from that bipolar action gives birth
to something—like electricity. (60)

———

I attach even more importance to the
spectator than to the artist. (42)

———

The art historian and critic have a right and
duty to analyze and interpret art and artists. ...
Often the artist is the last man to realize
what he has done. (46)

———

They [art critics] are parasites, parasites
on the artist. The collector who buys
paintings is a parasite of the painter.
They are all parasites, dealers, collectors,
museum, and art critics are all parasites.
They live like lice on the artist. (80)

———

The danger is in pleasing an immediate public
that comes around you and takes you in. …
Instead of that, you should wait for fifty years
or a hundred years for your true public. That
is the only public that interests me. (29)

———

I believe that a picture, a work of art,
lives and dies just as we do. That is, it lives
from the time it's conceived and created, for
some fifty or sixty years, it varies, and
then the work dies. And that is when
it becomes art history. (72)

———

After a work has lived almost the life
of a man—twenty or forty years, it doesn't
matter the number of years—comes a period
when that work of art, if it is still looked at
by onlookers, is put into a museum. ... That's
why I say the life and death of a work of
art—death meaning posterity, meaning
art history. (60)

———

I don't see why we give to posterity this
prerogative of deciding what is good and
what is bad. Especially as this posterity
changes every fifty years. Nor do I see why
contemporaries can judge better. The idea
of judgment should disappear. (27)

———

Different ages analyze works of art according to their own suppositions; the Greeks had one set of criteria, the Romantics stressed other factors, the 20th century still others. All these approaches have their place but none of them is correct. (32)

———

It is we who discovered Raphael and decided that he was a great artist. In his own time he was probably just another artist. (8)

———

The word "belief" is another error. It's like the word "judgment," they're both horrible ideas, on which the world is based. I hope it won't be like that on the moon! (68)

I like the word "belief." In general when
people say, "I know," they don't know,
they believe. ... To live is to believe,
that's my belief. (28)

———

The modern artist must hate Picasso in
order to make something new, just as Courbet
hated Delacroix. The son must hate the father
in order to be a good son. Such hatred seems
to be the only means of producing that
necessary reaction against the achievements
of the previous period. (8)

———

The moment of crisis for an artist is around the age of forty. It is then that he should change himself completely or be resigned to copying himself. (15)

———

I was really trying to invent, instead of merely expressing myself. … My intention was always to get away from myself, though I knew perfectly well that I was using myself. Call it a little game between "I" and "me." (53)

———

Even if I don't believe there's too much in what I say, I don't mind even being made a fool of myself by myself. (58)

Art is produced by a succession of individuals expressing themselves; it is not a question of progress. Progress is merely an enormous pretension on our part. (16)

———

An abstract painting may not look at all "abstract" in 50 years. (16)

———

The word "anti" annoys me a little, because whether you're anti or for, it's two sides of the same thing. And I would like to be completely—I don't know what you say—nonexistent, instead of being for or against. (59)

———

What is a work of art? Your whole life,
a producing mind, can be a work of art.
Even *action* can be art. Even a grocer can
be—*can be*—an artist. (35)

———

Aesthetics is not a matter of beauty and
ugliness. Formal analysis does not bring us
closer to any final answer. (32)

———

Tradition is the great misleader because it's
too easy to follow what has already been
done—even though you may think
you've giving it a kick. (53)

The abstract expressionists don't shock anybody. The only shocking thing these days is the stupidity of Russian painting. (38)

———

There is nothing static about my manner of working. I am never deceived into thinking that I have at length hit upon the ultimate expression. In the midst of each epoch I fully realize that a new epoch will dawn. (4)

———

I don't think oil painting will last another 50 years. It'll cease to be, like illuminated manuscripts. New forms of life and new techniques are springing up. (65)

———

Already new techniques have made their
appearance and one can foresee that in the
same way, as in the invention of new instru-
ments in Music changes the sensitivity of a
whole epoch, light effects on new materials
may become, among other things, a
tool for the new artist. (41)

———

As for museums, they'll probably go on
collecting things, but they may store them on
tape. You may be able to see an art show in
Tokyo simply by pushing a button. (65)

———

I really believe that the young artist of
tomorrow will resent the naiveté of such a
dilemma as "figurative" or "non-figurative."
Like Alice in Wonderland he will pass through
the looking glass of the retina to reach
deeper mines of expression. (44)

———

It may be that great art can only come
out of conditions of resistance, out of a state
of war which forces the artist into an attitude
of dedication that is almost religious and does
not need the acceptance of society. (59)

———

Art is a habit-forming drug, that's all it is,
for the collector, for the artist, for anybody
connected with art. (60)

———

Art doesn't interest me. Artists interest me. (55)

———

I act like an artist although I'm not one. (76)

———

I'm nothing else but an artist, I'm sure,
and delighted to be. (59)

———

Painting

It's believed that painting is addressed to the retina. That was everyone's error. The retinal shudder! Before, painting had other functions: it could be religious, philosophical, moral. (68)

———

For the last hundred years we have been in an era of painting for the sake of painting such as was not known two hundred, nor yet four hundred years back. Fra Angelico, for instance, had no idea of painting for its own sake: he aimed merely at glorifying religion. Recently, however, we are almost totally absorbed in a love of brush stroke. Emotion, even, is today subordinated to the hand and everything is concentrated in the success of the brush stroke. (8)

———

For me, painting is out of date. It is a waste
of energy, no good engineering, not practical.
We have photography, the cinema, so many
other ways of expressing life now. (10)

———

I would rather be shot, kill myself or
kill someone than paint again. (13)

———

I believe we are returning to a painting
of a non-retinal approach. Pop Art painting
has passed the retinal barrier, and the
intellect wants to come in. (63)

———

Of course, there will always be painters. But for me, there is no religion for the life in it anymore. I am unable to see who may be the geniuses of tomorrow now working their way upward. To me they seem to be going backward, not progressing. (10)

———

The word forward implies the acceptance of progress, and progress, of course, does not exist in art that I know of. There is no progress in art. (18)

———

I have nothing against painting, believe me;
I don't want to demolish everything; everyone
has the right to live and to do as he pleases.

(69)

———

I myself haven't given up painting,
I'm just not painting now, but if I have an
idea tomorrow, I will do it. I want to live in
whatever way I like. One is not free if one is a
painter. The public expects a painter to paint.
Most painters paint by habit. (20)

———

I simply stopped [painting] because I didn't
have something more to say at the time.
I had run out of ideas; ideas don't come
as easily as all that. (72)

———

All painters should be pensioned at 50 and
compelled to quit work. The government
should see to it that the retired painters live on
their pensions, and do not work clandestinely
and secretly. Another sideline job for the
prohibition enforcement department. (7)

———

I cannot explain my paintings. Either one
grasps their purport or one doesn't. (4)

———

I was becoming a professional painter,
and professionalism is always the death of art.
The old masters were professionals, which
means they were one-man factories.
Art isn't made in factories. (11)

———

A painting has a very short life—from
when it's painted until the perfume of it has
disappeared. A rather short time—maybe
years, or even not years. I think it's very
important that paintings live like flowers—
they bloom and fade. (21)

———

Painting should not be only retinal or visual;
it should have to do with the gray matter
of our understanding. (28)

———

My paintings are a challenge to the intellect
or more exactly the *esprit*. ... When I said that
I wished to put painting at the service of the
mind I was using the word *esprit* in all its
meanings: intellect, spirit, wit. (32)

———

There is a tension set up between my
titles and the pictures. The titles are not the
pictures nor vice versa, but they work
on each other. (32)

———

Before, painting was esoteric and the Cubist
revolution did not have the repercussions
that it had fifty years later. ... Everything
is modified with anecdote. (33)

———

I think it is the individual who remains
important in the work of art. Each painter,
or each artist is, in spite of everything, the
deus ex machina of the question. (42)

———

You know, to be a painter is to copy and
multiply the few ideas one has had now and
then. It's to exhibit life by one's hand.
That's what makes a painter. (15)

———

Each morning a painter, on waking, needs apart from his breakfast, a whiff of turpentine. (42)

———

The successful painter must produce—he paints apples, more apples and always apples. It's extremely annoying. (27)

———

In art there is no such thing as perfection. And a creative lull occurs always when artists of a period are satisfied to pick up a predecessor's work where he dropped it and attempt to continue what he was doing. (16)

———

When on the other hand you pick up something from an earlier period and adapt it to
your own work an approach can be creative.
The result is not new, but it is new insomuch
as it is a different approach. (16)

———

When you try to analyze a painting
using words, you can only manage a very
questionable approximation, worse than
questionable, because after all, painting and
art in general, especially visual art, is a
language in itself, a visual language
instead of a spoken language. (72)

———

My attitude towards Art is that of an atheist towards religion. (13)

———

All good painters have only about five masterpieces to their name. The others are not vital. The five have the force of shock. Shock is good. If I've done five good things, it's enough. (30)

———

One cannot change style more than two or three times in a very full life. (27)

———

You must be able to contradict yourself with alacrity which is not at all a bad thing. I am in favor of contradiction, and particularly with oneself. (42)

———

As it happens, I have produced extremely little because I couldn't repeat myself. The idea of repeating, for me, in an artist, is a form of masturbation. (42)

———

Silence is the best production that one can make because one doesn't sign it. Everyone benefits, one knows what silence is. It exists and it is even propagated faster than electric light. It's interesting in that way. (42)

———

It seems quite possible that, nauseated by the smell and the cult of oil paint, the artist might do away altogether with this five-century old technique, and its academic tyranny, so likely to limit his freedom of expression. (44)

———

In fact the principal factor in art today is boredom. (73)

———

Dada and Surrealism

In the beginning, the [C]ubists broke up form without even knowing they were doing it. Probably the compulsion to show multiple sides of an object forced us to break the object up—or even better to project a panorama that unfolded different facets of the same object. (53)

———

It was only later we discovered that we were breaking something: it didn't make a noise when it happened. (53)

———

[I first heard about Dada] in [Tristan]
Tzara's book, *The First Celestial Adventure of Mr.*
Fire Extinguisher. I think he sent it to us, to me
or to [Francis] Picabia, rather early, in 1917,
I think, or at the end of 1916. It interested
us but I didn't know what Dada was,
or even that the word existed. (68)

———

Dada is nothing. For instance the
Dadaists say that everything is nothing:
nothing is good, nothing is interesting,
nothing is important. ... It is very
contradictory. (6)

———

Anything that seems wrong is right for a true Dadaist. As soon as a thing is produced they are against its production. It is destructive, does not produce, and yet in just that very way it is constructive, do you see? (6)

———

Dada was an extreme protest against the physical side of painting. It was a metaphysical attitude. It was intimately and consciously involved with "literature." It was a sort of nihilism to which I am still very sympathetic. (16)

———

It was a way to get out of a state of mind—to avoid being influenced by one's immediate environment, or by the past; to get away from clichés—to get free. (16)

———

I was in sympathy with Dadaism, which was not just a matter of art or literature; it was born of World War I. The war marked a break from the ancient world; people were glad it did. (17)

[Dadaism] introduced a chapter of humor into art history. It said one mustn't always cry and think in terms of going to heaven. One must laugh at oneself. Dadaism said no to the pompous. It was not pessimistic, it said no to no. It was based on humor. (26)

———

Dada [was] very serviceable as a purgative. (14)

———

I was never a real Dadaist. (54)

———

[In response to the question of whether or not Dada still existed:] Well yes. Perhaps in some of the new generation. Do you know the works of Rauschenberg and Jaspers [Jasper Johns]? Perhaps there, where the intention is not so much just in technique. (35)

———

Pop art is just a "second wind" of Dada. (54)

———

Surrealism took a small amount from Dada at its inception, then became a positive form of development in its own right, based on the dream, the subconscious, fantasy. The Surrealists were more interested in aesthetics than life. (17)

———

The entire period from Courbet and Delacroix, through the Impressionists, Pointillists, Fauves, Cubists, was preoccupied with "retinal" vision. What was important was not the apple—not subject matter in itself—but the way in which it was painted. There was nothing behind the apple. The visible stopped at the canvas and the eye. The great asset of the Surrealists was that they reintroduced the use of "gray matter," both in the spectator and the artist. (17)

———

If I had the chance to take an antiretinal attitude, it unfortunately hasn't changed much; our whole century is completely retinal except for the Surrealists. (68)

———

With regard to painting, one can say
that Surrealism aimed at the rehabilitation
of the subconscious. (17)

———

Pure chance interested me as a way of
going against logical reality: to put something
on a canvas, on a bit of paper, to associate
the idea of a perpendicular thread a meter
long falling from the height of one meter
onto a horizontal plane, make its own
deformation. This amused me. (68)

———

It's always the idea of "amusement"
which caused me to do things. (68)

———

[I used chance] to get away from things already worked out. A real expression of the subconscious through chance. Your chance. If I make a throw of the dice, it will never be like your throw—meaning that is a marvelous expression of your subconscious. (60)

———

Fundamentally, the reason Surrealism survived is that it wasn't a school of painting. It isn't a school of visual art, like the others. It isn't an ordinary "ism," because it goes as far as philosophy, sociology, literature, etc. (68)

———

The great thing about Breton, I have not known a man who had a greater capacity for love. (74)

———

The Readymades

Readymade was from the beginning an invented word that I took to designate a work of art which isn't one. (41)

———

A readymade is a work of art without an artist to make it, if I may simplify the definition. (79)

———

It starts from a humoristic formula which is a necessary foundation of the readymade. It must not be a serious thing; the gaiety of the choice must intervene. (42)

———

When I put a bicycle wheel on a stool, the fork down, there was no idea of a "readymade" or anything else. It was just a distraction. I didn't have any special need to do it, or any intention of showing it, or describing anything. No, nothing like that. (68)

———

The main point [of the readymade] was disorientation for the spectator as it was for myself when I did it. Then surprise comes in as an element, connotation, meaning according to the observer's imagination. ... In other words, my reactions were not to be his reactions at all. (48)

———

It may be [that] it [*Bicycle Wheel*] is no longer a work of art, and if it is so I am delighted to have tried to do something to destroy art, if you want to say, and succeeded. (48)

———

I'm not at all sure that the concept of the readymade isn't the most important single idea to come out of my work. (53)

———

I don't want to destroy art for anybody else but myself, that's all. (48)

———

Museums will never be filled with readymades; but carried to an extreme of reason every picture is a readymade. (32)

———

There is always something "readymade"
in a picture; you don't make the brushes; you
don't make the colors; you don't make the
canvas. So going further, in removing everything, even the hand, you arrive at the "readymade." There is nothing left which is made.
Everything is "readymade." … It is a natural
consequence of following one's reasoning
to a logical conclusion. (78)

———

Everybody [can make a readymade], but I
don't attach any value—I mean commercial
value or even artistic value—to it. Hardly
anybody would do it for the sake
of doing it. (36)

———

If we accept the idea that trying not to define art is a legitimate conception, then the readymade can be seen as a sort of irony, or an attempt at showing the futility of trying to define art, because here it is, a thing that I call art ... it's a form of denying the possibility of defining art. (36)

It is not the idea just of a work of art at all, it's the idea that it was chosen, it's sacred because chosen. (42)

The choice of the readymade is always based on visual indifference and, at the same time, on the total absence of good or bad taste. (68)

In other words, they were not chosen because they looked nice or were artistic or in conformity to my taste. And that was the difficulty of choosing something, because the minute you choose something, generally, you are valuing the artistic facets of it or aesthetic essence of it. (60)

———

I don't choose them for their beauty. Beauty is terrible because we accept it and it becomes commonplace and comfortable. "Ugly" doesn't mean anything either, because it is just beauty with a minus sign. (67)

———

What interested me too was to give it a kind of flag or a color that did not come out of a tube of paint. I obtained this color by writing a phrase on the readymade in question, which had to be of poetic essence, and often without normal meaning. (42)

———

It's not the visual question of the readymade that matters, it's the simple fact that it exists. It can exist in your memory. You don't need\to look at it. … Visuality is no longer a question. … It is completely gray matter. It is no longer retinal. (78)

———

But one doesn't contemplate it like a picture.
The idea of contemplation disappears
completely. (78)

———

There's a danger of making too many
[readymades], since, you know, anything
however ugly it may be, however indifferent,
will become pretty after forty years. Rest
assured. So that's very worrying as regards
the actual idea of the readymade. (78)

———

Anything becomes beautiful if you look
at it long enough. (76)

———

I realized very soon the danger of repeating indiscriminately this form of expression and decided to limit my production of readymades to a small number yearly. I was aware at that time, for the spectator even more than for the artist, art is a habit-forming drug, and I wanted to protect my readymades against such a contamination. (48)

———

It doesn't take a long time to choose a snow shovel from the hardware shop, even so, you have to think and put a word on it, and it's half poetry and half plastic. (43)

———

It [the readymade] means "completely finished," like off-the-peg garments. (78)

———

[The readymade] was a sort of conclusion or consequence of dehumanization of the work of art. (28)

———

The readymades inspire no feeling whatever. It is hard to maintain this. I will keep something around for a long time; then, to my horror, it starts looking beautiful. Out it goes! That damned Hérisson [Bottle Rack] has become a great trial. It has begun to look too good. (67)

———

I threw the bottle rack and the urinal into their faces as a challenge and now they admire them for their aesthetic beauty. (52)

I don't like the word "anti." [The readymades] are anart, or non-art. I don't look at them. I think about them. (67)

I have always been disturbed by the uniqueness conferred upon painted art works, and that is why I saw them [editioned copies] as a solution offered by others to my need of escaping this dead-end and giving back to the readymades the freedom of repetition that they had lost. (77)

If you make an edition of eight Readymades, like a sculpture, like a Bourdelle or you name it, that is not overdoing it. There is something called "multiples," that go up to one hundred and fifty, two hundred copies. Now, there I do object because that's getting really too vulgar in a useless way, with things that could be interesting if they were seen by fewer people. (78)

———

I live what I am. This is what you call taking your life for a work of art. In other words, I just took the oil paint from the canvas and put it into my life instead. I used it to paint myself, in breathing and jumping, I'm my own living readymade, so to speak. (64)

———

The fact that [the readymades] are
regarded with the same reverence as objects
of art probably means I have failed to solve
the problem of trying to do away
entirely with art. (79)

———

The curious thing about the readymade
is that I've never been able to arrive at a
definition or explanation that fully satisfies
me. There's still magic in the idea, so
I'd rather keep it that way. (53)

———

Chess

From my close contact with artists and chess players I have come to the personal conclusion that while all artists are not chess players, all chess players are artists. (25)

———

I started playing chess with my brothers at thirteen, but not seriously. I'm a good player now, but there are two hundred like me in New York. (31)

———

If you start out playing chess when you are young, you'll still play chess when you grow old and die. It's a passion that accompanies you to your grave. It happened to me and very likely helped me to achieve what I wanted. (61)

———

I am still a victim of chess. It has all the
beauty of art—and much more. It cannot
be commercialized. Chess is much purer
than art in its social position. (22)

———

Chess in itself is a hobby, is a game. Everybody
can play chess. But I took it very seriously and
enjoyed it because I found some common
points between chess and painting. (28)

———

Chess has the visual possibilities of art.
It is a mechanistic sculpture that presents
exciting plastic values. (32)

———

When you play a game of chess, it is like designing something or constructing some mechanism of some kind by which you win or lose. The competitive side of it has no importance. The thing itself is very plastic. That is probably what attracted me to the game. (28)

It's mechanical sculpture, and with chess one creates beautiful problems; and that beauty is made with the head and hands. Besides, it's purer, socially, than painting, for you can't make money out of chess, eh? (30)

Chess has become a drug. (24)

If you know the game you can feel that the bishop is like a lever. It incites a whole new pattern when moved. There is a mental end implied when you look at the formation of the pieces on the board. (32)

―――――

The transformation of the visual aspect to the gray matter is what always happens in chess and what should happen in art. (32)

―――――

I am not of master caliber [as a chess player]. For that, eight hours a day, nine hours a day are necessary. One must devote one's life to chess to be a good player. (57)

―――――

I'm not a chess player in the sense you mean of a great chess player. There are only a few in the world. ... I was a good amateur and still am but there's nothing professional about my chess. (64)

———

I will even make some brilliant moves. But toward the end I may be at the mercy of an oversight or a mistake. (34)

———

In chess when you speak of a beautiful achievement in a problem it comes out of an abstract thinking and ends in a physical shaping of a king doing this or a queen doing that. As if it were giving life to an abstract thing. (14)

———

Objectively, a game of chess looks very much like a pen-and-ink drawing, with the difference, however, that the chess player paints with black-and-white forms already prepared instead of inventing forms as does the artist. (25)

———

Chess is a sport. A violent sport. This detracts from its most artistic connection. … It's a sad expression though—somewhat like religious art—it is not very gay. If it is anything, it is a struggle. (47)

———

The beautiful combinations that people invent in chess are only Cartesian after they are explained—in other words, you cannot see them coming at all. And yet when it's explained there is no mystery. It's a pure, logical conclusion, and it cannot be refuted. (60)

———

Beauty in chess is closer to beauty in poetry; the chess pieces are the block alphabet which shapes thoughts; and these thoughts, although making a visual design on the chessboard, express their beauty *abstractly*, like a poem. (25)

———

Literary Influences

My only interest [in being influenced by
literature] was to get something which was
not thought of before. (14)

———

[Jean-Pierre] Brisset and [Raymond] Roussel
were the two men in those years whom
I most admired for their delirium
of imagination. (16)

———

[François] Rabelais and [Alfred] Jarry are
my gods, evidentially. They were an example
to me of what could be unserious and yet
express things that were not completely
the lowest form of art. (68)

———

Poetry is a matter of association—give words their necessary freedom, let them reverberate.

(32)

———

[Roussel's] game with words had a hidden meaning. But the obscurity of these word games had nothing Mallarméan, nothing Rimbaudesque. It's an obscurity of another kind. (27)

———

My ideal library would have all Roussel—Roussel, Brisset, perhaps Lautréamont and Mallarmé. Mallarmé was the great figure. This is the direction in which art should turn to an intellectual expression rather than an animal expression. (14)

———

I agree that insofar as they recognize the primacy of change in life I am influenced by [Henri] Bergson and [Friedrich] Nietzsche.
(32)

———

I have the complete set of Lewis Carroll's works; I do feel that his imaginative scope, and his ability to be irreverent toward the so-called reality of things, have a connection to my attitude. Perhaps it is fair to say that this similarity may denote a chess player's frame of mind. (32)

———

We must realize the way the mind works
and beware of abstract words. I do not believe
that words such as reality and truth have
any meaning. (32)

———

There are things I never read, which I never
will read. Like [Marcel] Proust; in the end
I never read him. (68)

———

The Viennese logicians worked out a system
wherein everything is, as far as I understood
it, a tautology, that is, a repetition of premises.
In mathematics, it goes from a very simple
theorem to a very complicated one, but
it's all in the first theorem. (68)

———

So, metaphysics; tautology; religion; tautology: everything is tautology, except black coffee because the senses are in control. (68)

———

I like words in a poetic sense. Puns for me are like rhymes. (53)

———

[Roussel] puns a lot. Puns are considered very low, low, low everywhere, in English as well as in French. And he was using a low pun, not ever a good pun. (60)

———

Commercialization in Art

A hundred years ago, there were a few collectors, a few painters, a few critics, a world of art by itself. Now it is the layman's world. He has the right to say, "This painting is no good. I won't buy it and if I don't buy it, it is a bad painting, if I decide it is not worth anything." So that makes the whole thing entirely different and uninteresting to me. (20)

———

It is even worse in Europe than here. At least people here buy paintings for the sake of buying them and looking at them, while in Europe most collectors, except a few, merely buy to sell again. It is a commercial proposition. It is an investment. (20)

———

Artists, once having found a formula for painting, have used it for making money, selling their stuff like so many beans. (8)

———

Although much money has been derived from widespread sales, posterity will never see a great deal of the work we rave about because of the too frequent use of bad pigments. (8)

———

Since the creation of a market for paintings, everything has changed radically in the field of art. Look at how they produce. Do you think they like that, and enjoy painting fifty times, a hundred times the same thing? Not at all, they are not even producing paintings but cheques. (15)

———

[Art dealers can be] very good and very bad
at the same time. ... There are good dealers
and bad dealers, like everything else. It's a
very curious form of parasitism; instead
of being a bother, it's an enhancer. (60)

———

There seem to be some dealers in New York
who have taste and look for things they love.
(8)

———

Dealers can ruin artists. And money, money,
money comes in and it becomes a
Wall Street affair. (31)

These things *sell* nowadays. The Impressionists and the Cubists did not sell. That's the difference. (35)

———

The visual arts through their close connection with the law of supply and demand have become a commodity. The work of art is now a currently monetized item, like soap and securities. (41)

———

One buys art as one buys spaghetti. (42)

———

The dollar and art shouldn't mix, but they do, and since you can't destroy money, money is destroying art. (45)

———

There are so many buyers and so many artists that the aesthetic part will become completely nonexistent because it will be completely levelled, from the bottom up. (55)

———

I would have to hate the mixture of art and money as water in your wine. It's a very good comparison because it dilutes into mediocrity. Water in wine. The bouquet disappears. (55)

———

I stopped painting in 1923 because there was too much commercialism. I did not like the mixture of money and art. I like the pure thing. I don't like water in wine. (57)

———

We have so many standards: the gold standard, the platinum standard, and now the burlap standard. It's surprising that a piece of cloth, a piece of burlap on a stretcher with a few nails, can bring such prices. (55)

———

The pitfalls [for artists] are extremely numerous and hidden for a young man of twenty. How is he to guess that making too much money is a sin? And that doesn't make him an artist either. He could be a great person in himself and be completely annihilated by accepting what society offers him. (55)

———

If you choose to be an artist, you're an artist and you'll have more pleasure being an artist than anything else. (64)

―――

If I had a choice of being a millionaire or an artist, I would choose to be an artist any time. (64)

―――

There's nothing more boring than money. (64)

―――

That's the trouble with artists now. In my day, we wanted to be outcasts, pariahs. Now they're all integrated into society. They have country houses, two cars, three divorces and five children. An artist has to turn out lots of paintings to pay for all that, hmm? (65)

―――

Today art is big business, a public enterprise in which the layman evaluates, with a cursory glance, the life work or a single major effort by an artist, yet they do not pretend to pass judgment on the conclusions of the scientist or mathematician. (19)

———

People condemn Modern Art, but offer nothing in its place. It is here: a part of this age. One might just as well scoff at aeroplanes and the radio. It all depends on how we use them. (19)

———

More than ever, money has taken the form of a divinity. Is it because God has diminished in importance? … It's a form of competition. After all we live in a competitive world. (42)

———

The great danger for the artist today is commercialization and mediocritization [sic] of his art. Instead of individuality and genius you tend to get mediocrity. There is a new name in the mail every day … more than 350 new artists a year. They can't all be good. (56)

———

My capital is time, not money. (24)

———

Philosophies of Life
and Death

Change and life are synonymous. We must realize this and accept it. Change is what makes life interesting. (32)

———

We must learn to forget the past, to live our own lives in our own time. (1)

———

The dead should not be permitted to be so much stronger than the living. (1)

———

Life in the United States was a lot more simple than in France, or than in Europe. Because there is a respect for the individual here that isn't found in Europe. (41)

———

New York is a work of art, a complete work of art. Its growth is harmonious, like the growth of ripples that come on water when a stone has been thrown into it. (1)

———

The American woman is the most intelligent woman in the world today—the only one that always knows what she wants and therefore always gets it. ... This wonderful intelligence ... is helping the tendency of the world today to completely equalize the sexes, and the constant battle between them in which we have wasted our best entries in the past will cease. (2)

———

The thing which has struck me most in this country, which has undoubtedly the most beautiful women, is the lack of really strong emotions in your men. An American, for instance, if he has to choose between an important business appointment and an engagement with the woman he loves, rings her up on the telephone. "Hello, dear," he says, "I can't see you today: I must go to the bank instead." To a Frenchman that seems very stupid. (5)

———

I understood, at a certain moment, that it wasn't necessary to encumber one's life with too much weight, with too many things to do, with what is called a wife, children, a country house, and automobile. (68)

———

I've never had more than two or three hundred dollars ahead of me. I've never gone without a meal. People always ask artists how they live. They don't have to live. They just breathe. (31)

———

Breathing is my prime preoccupation.
I am a *respirateur*. (66)

———

I remember a book called *The Right to Be Lazy*:
that right doesn't exist now. You have to
work to justify your breathing. (55)

———

I decided at age 20 that I couldn't be an
organized citizen. I went on a strict economy
plan, modest living quarters, no luxuries,
to make it last. And it has. (35)

———

I didn't have to sell to live. All my life I've
been able to live on very little money. (38)

———

I have always been intrigued with the idea
of starting a Home for Lazy Men. (32)

———

My interest has always been with the individual, rather than the group. The greatest
aspect of man is his imagination. Nothing
important has ever been done by a group. (32)

———

I don't understand anything about politics,
and I say it's really a stupid activity, which
leads to nothing. Whether it leads to communism, to monarchy, to a democratic republic,
it's exactly the same thing, as far as I'm
concerned. ... I don't go for politics. (68)

———

Painting is now dedicated the world over to propaganda—to subject matter. (12)

—

Both Fascism and Communism are bent on regimenting people, robbing them of their individuality. It is no atmosphere in which creative art can thrive. The zest, the joy, is gone. (12)

—

The society of today is more materialistic than it has ever been before. Democracy stands for comfort; the best machines and mattresses. (49)

—

God is the natural end of man's desire for proof and an absolute. Explanation through cause and effect comes from this same desire to prove things. But how can we say what is really cause and effect? We cannot learn much from these types of distinctions. (32)

———

Creation and invention are the essence of things. They are the only important actions we can perform. (32)

———

Logic may be necessary to communication, but it reflects only part of man. I see no reason for discarding it completely, but we should not have too great a reliance on it. (32)

———

Obviously there can be no solution when there is no problem. Problems are inventions of the mind. They are nonsensical. (24)

———

There is no finality; we build tautologically and get nowhere. (32)

———

I believe in life being the expression of an individual today. Even if in two hundred thousand years we will be a mass conglomeration of souls having to do everything that the other fellow does. I don't care for that society. (55)

———

[I'm] trying to make my life into a work of art itself instead of spending my life creating works of art in the form of paintings or sculptures. I now believe that you can quite readily treat your life, the way you breathe, act, interact with other people, as a picture, a tableau vivant or a film scene, so to speak. (72)

———

In spite of myself, I'm a meticulous man. (37)

———

I have a very great respect for humor[;] it's a protection which allows one to pass through all the mirrors. One can survive, even [attain] success. (62)

———

I was very happy when I discovered that
I could introduce humor into [my work].
And that was truly a period of discovery. The
discovery of humor was a liberation. (41)

———

It's not only about laughing. There's a humor
that is black humor which doesn't inspire
laughter and which doesn't please at all. (41)

———

Humor and laughter—not necessarily
derogatory derision—are my pet tools. This
may come from my general philosophy of
never taking the world too seriously—for
fear of dying of boredom. (53)

———

To play—that is best ... [Americans] are like children, like the French. They play with everything, baseball, business, invention, art, architecture. (3)

———

I hate serious living. Society is stupid. You were put on earth to work, it makes no sense. I mean why should you work, working is the enemy of living. (80)

———

Seriousness is something very dangerous. To avoid seriousness, humor must be introduced. (50)

———

If the religion of the Catholic church were invented today—it would be a huge joke. Burning incense; long robes, and the theatrics of invoking God. But it's not funny only because of history. (51)

———

The realization of the game-like nature of life is of greatest importance. We should not strive for absolutes, don't make truth of the rules, recognize that we play the game according to ruses as we see them now. (32)

———

My work has been an attempt to show that reason is less fruitful than we think. (32)

———

I find the laws of physics, such that they are,
such that they have taught us, aren't
inevitably the truth. (41)

———

I believe that it's possible to consider
the existence of a universe where these
laws would be extended, change a little bit,
precisely limited. And as a result, one immedi-
ately obtains some extraordinary and different
results which are certainly not far from the
truth because, after all, every hundred years
a new scientist comes along who changes
the laws, right? (41)

———

I've never believed in causality. Because you light a match and see a fire you consider that a law. It's a very nice word, *law*, but it has no deep validity. That's what I think. It's just a habit. (60)

———

Eroticism is a very dear subject in my life. … It's an animal thing that has so many facets that it's pleasing to use it as a tube of paint, so to speak, to inject in your productions. (37)

———

[Eroticism is] really a way to try to bring out in the daylight things that are constantly hidden—that aren't necessarily erotic—because of the Catholic religion, because of social rules. To be able to reveal them, and to place them at everyone's disposal—I think this is important because it's the basis of everything, and no one talks about it. (68)

———

I want to grasp things with the mind the way the penis is grasped by the vagina. (40)

———

A genius is not made by the mind itself. It is made by the onlooker. The public *needs* a top mind and makes it. Anything can be on top. Genius is an invention of man, just like God.

(70)

[First decide] whether you want to make a living or be a genius. You often have to be dead to be called a genius. (39)

You know that theoretically the revolution is due and you are impatient for it, but I am here to tell you that there won't be one. Revolutions are *démodé*. There is no real need for them. They did not use to have them. They are modern inventions. (23)

There is no freedom, it is purely a human invention … we're all slaves of something or free of something. (71)

———

The painter is a medium who doesn't realize what he is doing. No translation can express the mystery of sensibility, a word still unreliable, which is nevertheless the basis for painting or poetry, like a kind of alchemy. (33)

———

It is always the individual that interests me more than the movements which simply serve to group the young. (42)

———

What would history be without death? … The
destiny of a life cannot be understood until it
has reached its end—until the long and
derisive train of days that make it up have
been united into one single story, the ending
of which can no longer change. (75)

———

I have had an absolutely marvelous life. …
I had luck, fantastic luck. I never had a day
without eating, and I have never been rich
either. So, everything turned out well! (69)

———

Quite simply, I am waiting for death.
You have to realize that there comes an age
when you no longer need to do anything,
unless you want to. I don't want to. I don't
want to work or do something. I'm fine as I
am. I think life is so great when you have
nothing to do, no work. … Art questions are
of absolutely no interest to me now. (78)

———

Physiologically you're obliged to think
about it [death] from time to time, at my age,
when you have a headache or break your leg.
Then death appears. (68)

———

Despite yourself, when you're an atheist, you're impressed by the fact that you're going to completely disappear. I don't want another life, or metempsychosis. ... It would be much better to believe in all those things[;] you'd die joyfully. (68)

———

Death is an indispensable attribute of a great artist. ... His voice, his appearance, his personality—in short, his whole aura—intrudes such that his pictures are overshadowed. Not until all these factors have been silenced, can his work be known for its own greatness. (9)

———

Two years after my death, no one will
say anything more! (69)

———

There won't be any difference between when
I'm dead and now, because I won't know it.
(55)

———

I don't have any [regrets]. I really don't. I've
missed nothing. I have had even more luck at
the end of my life than at the beginning. (68)

———

Art never saved the world. It cannot. (73)

———

Besides, it's always the others who die. (81)

———

SOURCES

1. Duchamp, Marcel. "A Complete Reversal of Art Opinions by Marcel Duchamp, Iconoclast." *Arts and Decoration* 5 (September 1915): 427–28, 442.

2. Breuer, Bessie. "The Nude-Descending-a-Staircase Man Surveys Us." *New York Tribune*, September 12, 1915, sec. 4, 2.

3. Kreymborg, Alfred. "Why Marcel Duchamps [sic] Calls Hash a Picture." *Boston Evening Transcript*, September 18, 1915, 12.

4. "French Artists Spur on an American Art." *New York Tribune*, October 24, 1915, sec. 4, 2–3.

5. Greeley-Smith, Nixola. "Cubist Depicts Love in Brass and Glass: 'More Art in Rubbers Than in Pretty Girl.'" *Evening World*, April 4, 1916, 3.

6. Rex, Margery. "'Dada' Will Get You if You Don't Watch Out: It Is on the Way Here." *New York Evening Journal*, January 29, 1921.

7. Bulliet, C. J. *Chicago Evening Post*, January 11, 1927. Excerpted in Jennifer Gough-Cooper and Jacques Caumont, *Marcel Duchamp: Work and Life / Éphémérides on and about Marcel Duchamp and Rrose Sélavy, 1887–1968*, edited by Pontus Hultén (Cambridge: MIT, 1993).

8.   Eglington, Laurie. "Marcel Duchamp: Back in America,
     Gives Interview." *Art News* 32, no. 7 (November 18, 1933):
     10–11.

9.   Duchamp, Marcel. Interview with an unnamed reporter.
     Berkshire County Eagle (Pittsfield, MA), June 16, 1936.
     Excerpted in Gough-Cooper and Caumont, *Duchamp: Work
     and Life / Éphémérides*, June 16, 1936.

10. "Restoring 1,000 Glass Bits in Panels." *Literary Digest*
     (June 20, 1936): 20–22.

11. Miller, Arthur. "Painter Hits Art Theory." *Los Angeles Times*,
     August 16, 1936, 2.

12. Bulliet, C. J. Interview with Duchamp. *Chicago Daily News*,
     August 25, 1936. Excerpted in Gough-Cooper and Cau-
     mont, *Marcel Duchamp: Work and Life / Éphémérides*, August
     25, 1936.

13. "Art: Cubism to Cynicism." *Time*, August 31, 1936, 22.

14. "Notes from Interviews with James Johnson Sweeney, Feb-
     ruary 1943 through February 1947." Typescript, Duchamp
     Archives, Library of the Philadelphia Museum of Art.

15. Rougemont, Denis de. "Marcel Duchamp, mine de rien."
     Preuves (Paris), no. 204 (February 1968). Diary entries
     for Lake George, New York, August 3, 6, 7, and 9, 1945,
     43–47; selected entries excerpted and translated in Gough-
     Cooper and Caumont, *Marcel Duchamp: Work and Life /
     Éphémérides*, August 6, 1945.

16. Duchamp, Marcel. "Eleven Europeans in America." *Museum of Modern Art Bulletin* 13, nos. 4–5 (1946): 19–21, 37.

17. Norman, Dorothy. "Two Conversations: Marcel Duchamp and Tristan Tzara." *Yale University Library Gazette* (October 1985), 77–80. Norman reports that her conversation with Duchamp took place in the late 1940s.

18. Cited in Gough-Cooper and Caumont, *Marcel Duchamp: Work and Life / Éphémérides*, April 9, 1949; https://www .duchamparchives.org/pma/archive/component/MDP _B002_F022_001/.

19. Rose, Kenneth. *Daily News* (Los Angeles), April 23, 1949. Cited in Gough-Cooper and Caumont, *Marcel Duchamp: Work and Life / Éphémérides*, April 23, 1949.

20. Art Institute of Chicago, October 19, 1949. See Naomi Sawelson-Gorse, "The Art Institute of Chicago and the Arensberg Collection," in *One Hundred Years at the Art Institute: A Centennial Celebration. Museum Studies* 19, no. 1 (1993): 96–105.

21. K[rasse], B[elle]. "A Marcel Duchamp Profile." *Art Digest* 26, no. 8 (January 15, 1952): 24.

22. "A Family Affair." *Time*, March 10, 1952, 82.

23. Remarks delivered at a dinner party at the home of James Johnson Sweeney and his wife in New York on March 17, 1950, as reported by Henry McBride. Quoted in Gough-

Cooper and Caumont, *Marcel Duchamp: Work and Life /
Éphémérides*, March 17, 1950.

24. Sargeant, Winthrop. "Dada's Daddy." Life (April 28, 1952):
100–108.

25. Statement delivered at the annual meeting of the New
York State Chess Federation, Cazenovia, New York, August
30, 1952. Transcribed in Gough-Cooper and Caumont,
Marcel Duchamp: Work and Life / Éphémérides, August 30,
1952.

26. Duchamp, Marcel. Interview with Dorothy Norman. *Art in
America* 57, no. 4 (July–August 1969): 38. Norman indi-
cates that the interview with Duchamp took place in 1953.

27. Duchamp, Marcel. Interview with Alain Jouffroy, Paris,
November 24, 1954. Published as "Interview Exclusive
[avec] Marcel Duchamp: L'idée de jugement devrait dis-
paraître." *Arts* (Paris) 491 (November 24–30, 1954): 13.
Excerpts translated in Gough-Cooper and Caumont, *Marcel
Duchamp: Work and Life / Éphémérides*, November 24, 1954.

28. Sweeney, James Johnson, Marcel Duchamp, James Nelson,
eds. *Wisdom: Conversations with the Elder Wise Men of Our Day*
(New York: W. W. Norton, 1958), 97. According to Sweeney's introduction, the interview took place in late 1955.

29. Duchamp, Marcel. Interview with James Johnson Sweeney.
Philadelphia Museum of Art, August 3, 1955. Televised as
A Conversation with Marcel Duchamp, January 15, 1956. Excerpts

quoted in Gough-Cooper and Caumont, *Marcel Duchamp: Work and Life / Éphémérides*, January 15, 1956.

30. Chanin, A. L. "Then and Now." *New York Times Magazine*, January 22, 1956, 24–25.

31. Duchamp, Marcel. *New Yorker*, April 3, 1957, 25–27. Although not acknowledged in the magazine, this article was written by Calvin Tomkins.

32. Gould, Laurence S. Interview with Marcel Duchamp. "Marcel Duchamp." Senior thesis, Princeton University, 1958, i–xiii.

33. Duchamp, Marcel. Interview, October 2, 1958, for a book entitled *Ces Peintres vous parlent*, published by L'Œil du Temps in 1964. See Gough-Cooper and Caumont, *Marcel Duchamp: Work and Life / Éphémérides*, October 2, 1958.

34. Roché, Henri-Pierre. "Souvenirs of Marcel Duchamp." In Robert Lebel, *Marcel Duchamp*, translated by George Heard Hamilton (New York: Grove Press, 1959), 83–84.

35. Tallmer, Jerry. "Marcel Duchamp at 72: A Toothbrush in a Lead Box—Would It Be a Masterpiece?" Interview conducted in 1959. Published in Daniel Wold and Edwin Faucher, eds., *The Village Voice Reader* (New York: Grove Press, 1963), 325–29.

36. Interview with George Heard Hamilton for BBC Radio, January 19, 1959. Published as "Mr. Duchamp, if you'd only known Jeff Koons was coming." *Art Newspaper*, no. 15

(February 1992): 13. Excerpts quoted in Gough-Cooper and Caumont, *Marcel Duchamp: Work and Life / Éphémérides*, January 19, 1959.

37. Duchamp, Marcel. Interview with Charles Mitchell, George Heard Hamilton, and Richard Hamilton. BBC Studios, London, September 1959. Transcript, Philadelphia Museum of Art, 13 pp. (unnumbered).

38. "Art Was a Dream … " *Newsweek*, November 9, 1959, 118–19.

39. Bright, Barbara. "Geniuslike Artist Has World Against Him, Says Duchamp." *Atlanta Constitution*, April 13, 1960, 22.

40. Steefel, Jr., Lawrence D. *The Position of Duchamp's "Glass" in the Development of His Art*. PhD dissertation submitted May 1960, Princeton University; published by Garland Press in 1977.

41. Duchamp, Marcel. Interview with Guy Viau. "Changer de nom, simplement." Canadian Radio Television, July 17, 1960; published in Fin, no. 5 (June 2000): 8–15; translated by Sarah Skinner Kilborne and published as *To Change Names, Simply*, in Tout-Fait: Marcel Duchamp Studies Online Journal 2, no. 4 (January 2000).

42. Duchamp, Marcel. Interview with Georges Charbonnier. Radio Française, October 7, 1960, broadcast on December 16, 1960. See entries in Gough-Cooper and Caumont, *Marcel Duchamp: Work and Life / Éphémérides*, October 7,

1960; December 9, 1960; December 16, 1960; December 17, 1960; December 30, 1960; January 6, 1961; and January 13, 1961.

43. Duchamp, Marcel. Script Log and Interview with Mike Wallace. December 12, 1960 (televised January 18, 1961). Transcribed in Naomi Sawelson-Gorse, "On the Hot Seat: Mike Wallace Interviews Marcel Duchamp." *Art History* 23, no. 1 (March 2000): 35–55.

44. Duchamp, Marcel. "Where Do We Go from Here?" Remarks delivered at a symposium moderated by Katherine Kuh, in which Louise Nevelson, Larry Day, and Theodoros Stamos participated. Philadelphia Collection of Art, March 20, 1961; three transcript pages. Duchamp Archive, Philadelphia Museum of Art.

45. Canaday, John. "Wither Art?" *New York Times*, March 26, 1961.

46. Camfield, William. Notes from an interview with Duchamp. New York, April 4, 1961. Typescript, Camfield Archive, Houston, Texas.

47. Brady, Frank R. "Duchamp, Art and Chess." *Chess Life* 16, no. 6 (June 1961): 168.

48. Duchamp, Marcel. Art of Assemblage Symposium. Museum of Modern Art, New York, October 19, 1961, moderated by William C. Seitz. Transcript, Museum of Modern Art Library, 1–43; published in *Essays on Assemblage (Studies in*

Modern Art) (New York: Museum of Modern Art, 1992), 124–59.

49. Duchamp, Marcel. Interview with Herbert Crehan for WBAJ-FM Radio, New York. Transcript published in *Evidence* (Toronto), no. 3 (Fall 1961): 36–39.

50. Duchamp, Marcel. Interview with Alain Jouffroy for an article in *Connaissance des Arts*. New York, December 8, 1961. See Gough-Cooper and Caumont, *Marcel Duchamp: Work and Life / Éphémérides*, December 8, 1961.

51. Duchamp, Marcel. Interview with Marvin Lazarus. New York, April 4, 1962. See Gough-Cooper and Caumont, *Marcel Duchamp: Work and Life / Éphémérides*, April 4, 1961.

52. Letter from Marcel Duchamp to Hans Richter, November 10, 1962. Quoted in Hans Richter, *Dada Art and Anti-Art* (New York: McGraw Hill, 1965). See Gough-Cooper and Caumont, *Marcel Duchamp: Work and Life / Éphémérides*, November 10, 1962.

53. Kuh, Katherine, and Marcel Duchamp. *The Artist's Voice: Talks with Seventeen Artists* (New York: Harper & Row, 1962), 81–93.

54. Steegmuller, Francis. "Duchamp: Fifty Years Later." *Show* 3, no. 2 (February 1963): 28–29.

55. Seitz, William. "What's Happened to Art? An Interview with Marcel Duchamp on Present Consequences of New York's 1913 Armory Show." *Vogue* 141, no. 4 (February 15, 1963): 110–13, 129–31.

56. "Duchamp Paints Uncle Sam as Top 'Moderns' Collector." *Utica Daily Press*, February 18, 1963.

57. Schonberg, Harold C. "Creator of 'Nude Descending' Reflects After Half a Century." *New York Times*, April 12, 1963.

58. Duchamp, Marcel. Interview with Colette Roberts. Spring 1963. Typescript, Marcel Duchamp Archives, Philadelphia Museum of Art, 1–15.

59. Roberts, Francis. Interview with Marcel Duchamp. October 13, 1963, Pasadena Art Museum. Published as "I Propose to Strain the Laws of Physics." *Art News* 67, no. 8 (December 1968): 46–47, 62–63.

60. Tomkins, Calvin. Interviews with Marcel Duchamp in 1964. Published as *Marcel Duchamp: The Afternoon Interviews* (New York: Badlands, 2013), 23–93.

61. Drot, Jean-Marie, dir. *Jeu d'échecs avec Marcel Duchamp*. Episode for the series L'Art et ses hommes, broadcast by RFT Paris, June 8, 1964. The film was later expanded and re-edited under the title *Marcel Duchamp: A Game of Chess*, Home Vision Entertainment, Chicago, 1987.

62. Duchamp, Marcel. Interview with Otto Hahn. "Marcel Duchamp." *L'Express* (Paris), July 23, 1964, 22–23. Excerpts were published in English in "Passport No. G255300," *Art and Artists* 1, no. 4 (July 1966): 7–11. See Gough-Cooper and Caumont, *Marcel Duchamp: Work and Life / Éphémérides*, July 23, 1964.

63. Duchamp, Marcel. Interview with George McCue. *St. Louis Post-Dispatch*, November 23, 1964. See Gough-Cooper and Caumont, *Marcel Duchamp: Work and Life / Éphémérides*, November 23, 1964.

64. Bell, Don. "A Conversation with Marcel Duchamp, New York, 1965." *Canadian Art* 4, no. 4 (Winter 1987): 55–59.

65. Glueck, Grace. "Duchamp Opens Display Today of 'Not Seen and/or Less Seen.'" *New York Times*, January 14, 1965.

66. "Pop's Dada." *Time*, February 5, 1965, 85.

67. Duchamp, Marcel. Interview with Don Morrison. *Minneapolis Star*, October 18, 1965. See Gough-Cooper and Caumont, *Marcel Duchamp: Work and Life / Éphémérides*, October 18, 1965.

68. Cabanne, Pierre. Interviews conducted with Marcel Duchamp in 1966. Later published as *Dialogues with Marcel Duchamp*, translated by Ron Padgett (New York: Viking Press, 1971).

69. Duchamp, Marcel. Interview with Pierre Cabanne. *Arts et Loisirs*, May 5, 1966. See Gough-Cooper and Caumont, *Marcel Duchamp: Work and Life / Éphémérides*, May 5, 1966.

70. Ashton, Dore. "An Interview with Marcel Duchamp." *Studio International* 171 (June 1966): 244–47.

71. Transcript of interview with Marcel Duchamp for the Arts Council of Great Britain. Interviewers included R. B. Kitaj, Richard Hamilton, William Coldstream, Robert Melville,

and David Sylvester. Conducted at the studio of Richard Hamilton, London, June 19, 1966, 1–36.

72. Duchamp, Marcel. Interview with Jean Antoine. Duchamp's Neuilly studio, Summer 1966. "Life Is a Game; Life Is Art." *Art Newspaper*, no. 27 (April 1993): 16–17.

73. Duchamp, Marcel. Interview with Claude Rivière. Cadaqués, France, September 8, 1966. Published as "Marcel Duchamp devant le pop'art." *Combat*, September 9, 1966. See Gough-Cooper and Caumont, *Marcel Duchamp: Work and Life / Éphémérides*, October 8, 1966.

74. Duchamp, Marcel. Interview on the subject of André Breton. Paris, October 5, 1966. Published as "André Breton: Les Hommes, Les Idees, Les Faits." *Arts et Loisirs*, no. 54 (October 5–11, 1966): 4–7. See Gough-Cooper and Caumont, *Marcel Duchamp: Work and Life / Éphémérides*, October 5, 1966.

75. Parinaud, André. "André Breton: Entretien avec Marcel Duchamp." Published in *Omaggio a Marcel Duchamp*, Galleria Schwarz, Milan, January 1967, 19–46.

76. Duchamp, Marcel. Interview with Jeanne Siegel. April 1967. Published in *Arts* 43, no. 3 (December 1968/January 1969): 21–22.

77. Lebel, Robert. "Marcel Duchamp maintenant et ici." *L'Œil* 149 (May 1967): 18–22, 77; reprinted in Lebel, *Marcel Duchamp* (Paris: Les Dossier Belfond), 119–30.

78. Duchamp, Marcel. "Marcel Duchamp Talking about Ready-mades: Interview with Philippe Collin, Galerie Givaudan, Paris, 21 June 1967," in Museum Jean Tinguely, Basel, exhibition catalog, 20 March–30 June 2002 (Ostfildern-Ruit: Hatje Cantz, 2002): 37–40.

79. Roberts, Francis. "I Propose to Strain the Laws of Physics." *Art News* 67, no. 8 (December 1968): 47.

80. Duchamp, Marcel. Unpublished interview with Arnold Eagle and Lewis Jacobs. Summer 1968, Cadaqués, Spain. Transcript, Getty Library, Los Angeles, California.

81. Words composed by Duchamp and inscribed on his tombstone ("D'ailleurs, c'est toujours les autres qui meurent" [Besides, it's always the others who die.]) in 1968, Cimetière Monumental, Rouen.

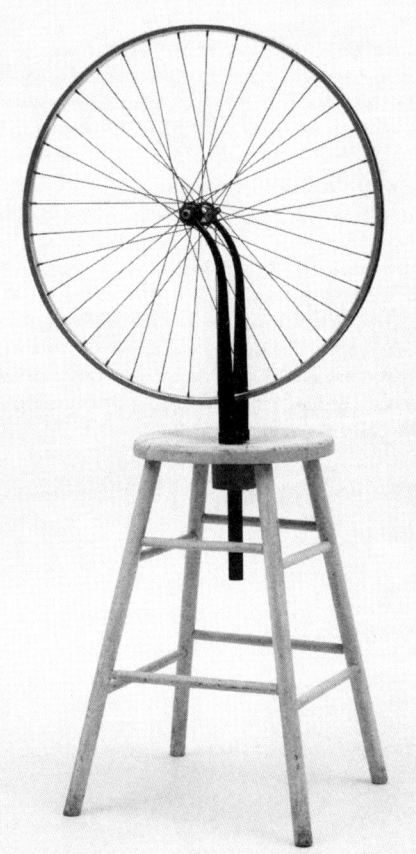

CHRONOLOGY

1887

July 28: Marcel Duchamp is born in Blainville-Crevon,
a small town in Normandy, about twenty-five miles
north of Rouen, where his father is the town notary.
His two older brothers will also go on to become
artists: Gaston, who takes the name Jacques Villon,
and Raymond, who changes his name to Raymond
Duchamp-Villon. Two sisters are born after Marcel—
one of whom, Suzanne, also becomes an artist.

1902

At the age of fifteen Duchamp paints his first pictures,
landscapes in an Impressionist style.

1904

Duchamp joins his brothers in Paris and begins his own
career as an artist. He studies briefly at the Julien
Academy in Paris.

1909

He exhibits his work for the first time: two paintings at the Salon des Indépendants in Paris and three works in the Salon d'Automne.

1910

Duchamp comes under the influence of Cézanne and the Fauves. He frequents the so-called Puteaux Group, weekly gatherings at the studios of his brothers in the western Paris suburb of Puteaux. The group includes poets and mathematicians as well as many Cubist painters.

1911

Duchamp begins painting in a Cubist style, particularly in a series of drawings and a painting depicting his brothers engaged in a game of chess.

1912

January: He paints *Nude Descending a Staircase No. 2*, which he submits to the Salon des Indépendants. Several members of the Cubist hanging committee object to the painting's title and style, which they consider too close to a rival movement, Futurism. They approach Duchamp's brothers to ask him to withdraw the picture—a momentous incident that Duchamp later explained "gave him a turn," causing him to question his career as an artist.

Summer: Duchamp undertakes an important two-month sojourn in Munich, Germany, where he begins compiling notes for a major project that he will not begin for another three years.

1913

February–March: *Nude Descending a Staircase No. 2* and three other paintings are exhibited in the Armory Show in New York. All four works sell, but *Nude* becomes a cause célèbre.

Duchamp finds a bicycle wheel on the street and brings it back to his studio.

1914

He works in an emphatically more mechanical style, painting two images of a chocolate grinder that he sees in a shop window in Rouen (where his family had moved in 1905).

He purchases a bottle rack that he brings back to his studio.

1915

June 15: Duchamp arrives in the United States. He stays for a brief period at the home of Walter Pach, an artist and writer whom he met in Paris, who encouraged him to come to New York.

He stays for a few months at the apartment of Louise and Walter Arensberg, who become his most dedicated and loyal patrons in New York. Over the next few years, he frequently attends gatherings at their home, which include a loose circle of artists and writers who eventually become known as New York Dada.

Shortly after his arrival, Duchamp sees the English word "readymade," a term used to describe clothing that is already made (as opposed to being custom-made to measure). It is the perfect term to categorize the two items he left back in his Paris studio, *Bicycle Wheel* and *Bottle Rack*. Duchamp and some friends purchase a snow shovel that he inscribes with the title *In Advance of a Broken Arm*. It is the first American readymade. He brings it back to his studio and hangs it from the ceiling.

Duchamp begins the actual execution of the work he has planned since 1912, *The Bride Stripped Bare by Her Bachelors, Even*, better known as *The Large Glass*. In 1923, he will leave the work intentionally incomplete.

1917

April–May: Under the pseudonym "R. Mutt," Duchamp submits a white porcelain urinal titled *Fountain* to the first exhibition of the Society of Independent Artists in New York. The work is refused, causing Duchamp and Walter Arensberg to resign from the organization.

1918–19

August: Duchamp departs for Buenos Aires, where he

will remain for ten months. He starts studying the game of chess seriously. In June 1919, he returns to Europe.

1920

With collector Katherine S. Dreier and artist Man Ray, he founds the Société Anonyme, Inc., the first museum in America devoted to the display of modern art.

1921

Back in New York, he collaborates with Man Ray on the publication of *New York Dada*.

1923

Duchamp returns to Europe, where he remains for the next eighteen years. He takes up chess seriously and enters into tournament play. He continues, however, to be actively involved in the world of art, advising collectors and helping to organize various exhibitions when requested.

1934

He publishes a facsimile edition of his notes for *The Large Glass.*

1936–41

He gathers images and prepares for the publication of an album of his art. It evolves into a suitcase containing miniature reproductions of his most important works. He titles the piece *Le Boîte-en-valise.*

1941

Escaping the ravages of war in Europe, Duchamp moves to New York. With occasional trips back to France, he remains in New York to the end of his life.

1943–51

Duchamp meets Brazilian sculptor Maria Martins, with whom he falls in love. She becomes the subject of an environmental tableau that he works on in secrecy for the next twenty years.

1945

March: A special issue of the Surrealist magazine *View* is
 devoted to Duchamp.

1954

Duchamp marries Alexina (Teeny) Sattler. She had been
 previously married to Pierre Matisse, son of Henri
 Matisse, who had become an art dealer in New York.

The collection of Louise and Walter Arensberg, including forty-three works by Duchamp, is given to the
 Philadelphia Museum of Art. *The Large Glass*, owned
 by Katherine S. Dreier, is also bequeathed to the
 museum, and Duchamp helps install it there.

1959

The first major monograph on Duchamp by Robert
 Lebel is published in Paris, followed by an American
 edition later that year.

1963

October–November: The first major retrospective of Duchamp's work, organized by noted curator Walter Hopps, opens at the Pasadena Museum of Art.

1968

Summer: Duchamp spends the summer months with his wife Teeny vacationing in the coastal town of Cadaqués in Spain.

October 2: Marcel Duchamp dies at the age of eighty-one in his studio in Neuilly, France.

1969

July: *Étant donnés*, the secret artwork inspired by Maria Martins, is installed in a small gallery near the Arensberg Collection at the Philadelphia Museum of Art.

ACKNOWLEDGMENTS

To Marcel Duchamp, whose words are the essence and core of this book, my deepest appreciation. Engaging with these ideas has been both an honor and an inspiration.

I extend my sincere gratitude to Francis Naumann, whose extraordinary research and curation provide the foundation of this publication. Your dedication to Duchamp's legacy ensures that his vision continues to challenge, provoke, and enrich the minds of generations to come.

My thanks as well to Séverine Gossart and the entire team at the Duchamp Association, whose participation was instrumental in bringing this project to life.

My sincere appreciation, as always, to the entire team at Princeton University Press, especially Michelle Komie, Christie Henry, Terri O'Prey, Cathy Slovensky, Jacqueline Poirier, Colleen Suljic, Laurie Schlesinger, Cathy Felgar, Jodi Price, Annie Miller, William Skurka, and Alexandria Leonard. Your professionalism and passion have been instrumental in bringing our projects to life over the years.

Special appreciation goes to editorial director Fiona Graham for her leadership in guiding this project and the entire ISMs series. My thanks also goes to Susan Delson for her insightful editorial input.

My sincere thanks as well to Taliesin Thomas and Steven Rodríguez for their continued support.

Above all, I give all my bottomless gratitude to my amazing wife, Abbey, and to my wonderful children, Justin, Ethan, Ellie, and Jonah, for their love and encouragement.

As always, I give endless love and thanks to my mother, Judith.

LARRY WARSH
JUNE 2025

ILLUSTRATIONS

Frontispiece: Man Ray, Marcel Duchamp, ca. 1920. Gelatin silver print. Image: 28.5 × 22.7 cm (11¼ × 8¹⁵⁄₁₆ in.); Mount: 39.8 × 32.7 cm (15¹¹⁄₁₆ × 12⅞ in.). Gilman Collection, Purchase, Ann Tenenbaum and Thomas H. Lee Gift, 2005 (2005.100.252). Image copyright © The Metropolitan. Image source: Art Resource, NY © Man Ray 2015 Trust / Artists Rights Society (ARS), NY / ADAGP, Paris 2025.

Page 118: Duchamp, Marcel, *Bicycle Wheel*, New York, 1951 (third version, after lost original of 1913). Metal wheel mounted on painted wood stool, 51 × 63.5 × 25 × 63.5 × 16 1/2 in. (129.5 × 63.5 × 41.9 cm). The Sidney and Harriet Janis Collection. Digital Image © The Museum of Modern Art / Licensed by SCALA / Art Resource, NY. © Association Marcel Duchamp / ADAGP, Paris / Artists Rights Society (ARS), New York, 2025.

Francis M. Naumann is an art historian, curator, and former art dealer specializing in the art of the Dada and Surrealist periods. He is the author of numerous articles and exhibition catalogs, including *New York Dada, 1915–25* (1994), considered to be the definitive history of the movement, and *Marcel Duchamp: The Art of Making Art in the Age of Mechanical Reproduction* (1999). His most recent books are *The Recurrent, Haunting Ghost: Essays on the Art, Life and Legacy of Marcel Duchamp* (2012), *MENTORS: The Making of an Art Historian* (2019), *Naomi Savage: Stretching the Limits of Photography* (2020), and *Peter Miller: Forgotten Woman of American Modernism* (2021). Naumann continues to write articles, books, and book reviews. He has recently completed "Impossible: The Love Affair between Marcel Duchamp and Maria Martins and the Artwork It Inspired," which will be published by Abbeville in 2026.

Marcel Duchamp (1887–1968) is considered the most influential artist of the twentieth century. He revised the very definition of art through his concept of the ready-made, the practice of selecting a commonplace, everyday object and elevating it to the status of art by the placement of his signature. He came to the attention of the general public through the display of his *Nude Descending a Staircase* at the Armory Show in 1913, a Cubo-Futurist painting whose subject critics found objectionable. Duchamp moved to the United States in 1915, and through his affiliation with artists who congregated at the apartment of Louise and Walter Arensberg during the years of World War I, he became part of a group that is today known as New York Dada. The most auspicious event to take place at this time was his submission, under the pseudonym of R. Mutt, of a men's urinal to an exhibition of the Society of Independent Artists in 1917, which they refused to display, causing a genuine scandal in the art world that reverberates to this day. He withdrew from artistic activities in 1923 and devoted a good part of the next twenty years to playing chess. He returned to the United States during the years of World War II, where he would remain for the rest of his life. His goal was to elevate art from its decorative qualities to a more cerebral experience, an idea that formed the basis of the Conceptual Art Movement of the 1960s.

Larry Warsh has been active in the art world for more than thirty years as a publisher and artist-collaborator. An early collector of Keith Haring and Jean-Michel Basquiat, Warsh was a lead organizer for the exhibition *Basquiat: The Unknown Notebooks*, which debuted at the Brooklyn Museum, New York, in 2015, and later traveled to several American museums. The founder of *Museums Magazine*, Warsh has been involved in many publishing projects and is the editor of the ISMs series and several other titles published by Princeton University Press, including *Jean-Michel Basquiat: The Notebooks* (2017), *Keith Haring: 31 Subway Drawings* (2021), *James Rosenquist: Collages, Drawings, and Paintings in Process* (2024), and *Wassily Kandinsky: The Sketchbooks* (2025). Warsh has served on the board of the Getty Museum Photographs Council and was a founding member of the Basquiat Authentication Committee until its dissolution in 2012.

ISMs

Larry Warsh, Series Editor

The ISMs series distills the voices of an exciting range of visual artists and designers into captivating, beautifully made books of quotations for a new generation of readers. In turn passionate, inspiring, humorous, witty, and challenging, these collections offer powerful statements on topics ranging from contemporary culture, politics, and race, to creativity, humanity, and the role of art in the world. Books in this series are edited by Larry Warsh and published by Princeton University Press in association with No More Rulers.

Duchamp-isms, Marcel Duchamp

Obrist-isms, Hans Ulrich Obrist

Calder-isms, Alexander Calder

Ono-isms, Yoko Ono

Minter-isms, Marilyn Minter

Fairey-isms, Shepard Fairey

Abramović-isms, Marina Abramović

JR-isms, JR

Holzer-isms: Artist's Edition, Jenny Holzer

Neshat-isms, Shirin Neshat

Judy Chicago-isms, Judy Chicago

Pharrell-isms, Pharrell Williams

Hirst-isms, Damien Hirst

Warhol-isms, Andy Warhol

Arsham-isms, Daniel Arsham

Abloh-isms, Virgil Abloh

Futura-isms, Futura

Haring-isms, Keith Haring

Basquiat-isms, Jean-Michel Basquiat